FOREWORD

Dear Reader,

Are you ready to get your thinking caps on to puzzle your way through this wonderful collection?

Young Writers' Little Riddlers competition set out to encourage young writers to create their own riddles. Their answers could be whatever or whoever their imaginations desired; from people to places, animals to objects, food to seasons. Riddles are a great way to further the children's use of poetic expression, including onomatopoeia and similes, as well as encourage them to 'think outside the box' by providing clues without giving the answer away immediately.

All of us here at Young Writers believe in the importance of inspiring young children to produce creative writing, including poetry, and we feel that seeing their own riddles in print will keep that creative spirit burning brightly and proudly.

We hope you enjoy riddling your way through this book as much as we enjoyed reading all the entries.

West Yorkshire Poets

Edited By Jenni Harrison

First published in Great Britain in 2018 by:

Young Writers
Remus House
Coltsfoot Drive
Peterborough
PE2 9BF
Telephone: 01733 890066
Website: www.youngwriters.co.uk

All Rights Reserved
Book Design by Ashley Janson
© Copyright Contributors 2018
SB ISBN 978-1-78896-478-4
Printed and bound in the UK by BookPrintingUK
Website: www.bookprintinguk.com
YB0361P

CONTENTS

Bramley St Peter's CE (VC) Primary School, Bramley

Isobelle French (7)	1
Tanatswa Laura Dube (7)	2
Finlay Cundy (7)	3
Isaiah Wamuhu	4
Logan Phillips-McKinley (7)	5
Morgan Wood	6
Ruby Mai Dean (6)	7
Lennon Preskey (7)	8
Scarlett Rose Owen (6)	9
Callum Haigh (7)	10
Edgar Cundy	11
Imogen Martin (7)	12
Anna Chandler (7)	13
Kyle Johnson (7)	14
Faye Durno (6)	15
Amelia-Leigh Varley	16
Sofie Gilchrist Osborne-Tucimova (7)	17
Lotachi Ikunna Oke-Nwosu (7)	18
Mollie Archer (7)	19
Xander Dennis McGurgan (7)	20
Poppy Spinks (6)	21
Dylan Withers (7)	22
Maya Vorlicky (7)	23
Adam Chmielewski (7)	24
Albert Henry Langton (7)	25
Logan Lewis Ivory Sutton (6)	26
Isabella Hemingway (6)	27
Ava Fox (6)	28
Cole Hyde (7)	29
Rosie Johnstone (6)	30
Ridley McManus (7)	31
Jack David Dennis Simpson (7)	32
Callum Brown (7)	33
Harry Oddy (6)	34
Luke Sheldon (7)	35
Millie-Rose Manning (6)	36
Lacey Baird (7)	37
Jack Thomas Albert Martin (7)	38
Finlay Cundy	39
Scarlet Davenport (6)	40
Kydon Temple (7), Charlie, Junior Smith (6) & Summer Welsh-Hayden	41

Gomersal Primary School, Gomersal

Woody Bainbridge (6)	42
Aliya Lane (5)	43
Eadie Chambers (5)	44
Leighton Ryan-Moorhouse (5)	45
Lily-Faye Allan (5)	46
Amelia Radforth (6)	47
Phoebe Tate (5)	48
Daniel Eric Booker (6)	49
Fraser Cowan (6)	50
Matilda May Mills (6)	51
Grace Emily Sheridan (5)	52
Harry Taylor (5)	53
Lucy Alexandra Brown (5)	54
Daniel Jackson (6)	55
Ben Hirst (6)	56
Noah Williams (6)	57
Harry Hall (5)	58
Max Holdsworth (5)	59
Owen Bramwell (5)	60
Isabelle Anders (5)	61
Lucie Jane Hobson (5)	62

Harry Bradley (6)	63
Isobel Brenda Hobson (5)	64
Paynten-Rose Shaw (6)	65
Edward James Griffiths (5)	66
Ethan Bryan (6)	67
Isla-Mai Elizabeth Hutton (5)	68

Healey Junior, Infant & Nursery School, Batley

Aamilah Bhana (6), Maya Ali & Ezan Abbas	69
Sameeha Rajah (6)	70
Miley Hanson-Senior (6)	71
Brooke Aubrey (6)	72
Zaid Ahmed Bhamji (5)	73
Aleeza Sultan (6)	74
Joseph Dylan Fenton (6)	75
Millie Ramsden (5)	76
Aadam Mahmood (5)	77
Lexie Leigh Trott (6)	78
Mason Massey (6)	79
Maxie Mir (6)	80
Zain Masood Lunat (5)	81
Ayaan Hussain (6)	82
Shahir Hussain Ahmed (5)	83
Delisia Docherty (6)	84
Rhys James Bingham (6)	85
Harris Tariq Hanif (6)	86
Ayaan Hussain (6)	87
Zaara Raja (5)	88
Maison Reynard (5)	89
Tillie Lowrie (6)	90
Riley Robin North (5)	91
Aqsa Younus Raja (5)	92

Home Schooled, Halifax

Fathima Hussain (7)	93
Zaynab Hussain (6)	94

Lidget Green Primary School, Lidget Green

Isa Tilal (7)	95
Aliyah Ali Hussain (7)	96
Zainab Batool (7)	97
Inaya Zara Moghul (7)	98
Muskaan Karim (6)	99
Israr Ali Shah (7)	100
Rayyan Nazir (7)	101
Rabiya Lateef (7)	102
Ahmad Raza (7)	103
Anmol Zeb (6)	104

Morley Newlands Academy, Morley

Nicole Getka (7)	105
Jack Smith (7)	106
Arissa Comrie (7)	107

Old Bank Junior Infant & Nursery School, Mirfield

Amie Bruniges (5)	108
Aleksander Kusek (6)	109
Jamie Lucas McKay (5)	110
Jasmine Baker (6)	111
Isaac Wood-Carney (5)	112
Harrison Joe Reynolds (6)	113
Alexandra Nagy (5)	114
Ethan Newby (5)	115
Isaac Whitfield (5)	116
Zach Shackleton (6)	117
Lexi Kim Main (6)	118
Lyla Buckley (5)	119
Eirlys Tomlinson (6)	120
Deakon Lucas Clayton (6)	121
Klisha Khan (6)	122
Ajie Humma (5)	123

Our Lady Of Lourdes Catholic Primary School, Sheepridge

Ryan Cornelius Lloyd (6)	124
Rhylee Phillips	125
Isaac Ashish Lazarus (6)	126
Nicol Katarzyna Domanska (5)	127
Nadia, Tianna Morgan, Amelia & Tomasz	128
Kyrelle Wood (6)	129

Paradise Primary School, Savile Town

Humayra Patel (8)	130
Aisha Bodhania (7)	131
Muhammad Muaaz Ismail (8)	132
Muhammad Soyab Patel (8)	133
Maryam Polli (8)	134
Umaama Ali (8)	135
Hafsa Tukur (8)	136
Fatima Moosa (8)	137
Maariyah Moosa (7)	138
Ariana Razaq (8)	139

Southroyd Primary School, Pudsey

Hannah Plant (6)	140
Dylan James Hall (6)	141
Henrikas Merkelis (5)	142
Eleanor Ighayere (6)	143
Lauren Bayly (6)	144

St Luke's CE Primary School, Bradford

Ruby Smith (9)	145
Mia Pheasby (10)	146
Sophie Grace Crabtree (9)	147
Ray Henry Mathieson (9)	148
Darnell Blythe (10)	149
Shola Henderson (9)	150
Daniel Senior (9)	151
Grace Mitchell (10)	152
Thomas Pashley (10)	153
Tyler Rhodes (9)	154
Daniela Megija Cielava (9)	155
Lily Robinson (10)	156
Rayaan Ahmed Ali (9)	157
Grace Hutchinson (10)	158

THE POEMS

Stab Power!

At the end of me, I feel as sharp
as a green, spiky thorn.
I'm not useful outside
because you don't need me.
Sometimes I'm silver
but I can be different colours.
I sound as quiet as a shampoo bottle.
I am a type of shiny cutlery.
You use often for mostly lunch and dinner.
I have four spikes
so you can stab me into your food.
Use me to eat breakfast
and maybe lunch or dinner.
What a handy gadget for eating.
What am I?

Answer: A fork.

Isobelle French (7)
Bramley St Peter's CE (VC) Primary School, Bramley

Flying High In The Sky

Don't break my string or I will escape.
Put me in the air so I can fly as fast as I can.
Do not pull me apart or I will never fly.
When you use me don't put me
on the ground because I won't fly again.
Let go of me because I love flying.
Hold me tight or I will fly as high as the sun.
Don't use me near an aeroplane.
What am I?

Answer: A kite.

Tanatswa Laura Dube (7)
Bramley St Peter's CE (VC) Primary School, Bramley

Wheel Speed!

Don't go too fast
because you might crash on me.
One type of me easily climbs
rocky, steep mountains.
I have wheels that grip.
Don't pedal too fast around corners.
Play with me in the park.
I have a chain so I can move.
What a terrific thing to go to school on.
What am I?

Answer: A bike.

Finlay Cundy (7)
Bramley St Peter's CE (VC) Primary School, Bramley

Zzz!

I feel like a comfy pillow.
Sleep on me so you can get some sleep.
I am soft and comfy.
You might need a ladder.
I'm good for sleeping.
If you feel tired, snuggle up on me.
I have four legs
but I cannot move.
Use me when the owls are awake.
What am I?

Answer: A bunk bed.

Isaiah Wamuhu
Bramley St Peter's CE (VC) Primary School, Bramley

High And Low

When I am wet you can't sleep on me.
Build me if you want to sleep on me.
When you are going to bed sleep on me.
I am made from wood from a tree.
I've got a quilt at the bottom.
I can come in yellow, green, red and blue.
I am high and low.
What am I?

Answer: A bunk bed.

Logan Phillips-McKinley (7)
Bramley St Peter's CE (VC) Primary School, Bramley

Smash It Up

I am made out of wood and titanium.
I am strong so you can use me.
I sound like this... *Bang, bang!*
Don't drop me on your toes or it will hurt.
I smell like titanium.
Sometimes you can use my back
and sometimes you can use my front.
What am I?

Answer: A hammer.

Morgan Wood
Bramley St Peter's CE (VC) Primary School, Bramley

Squishy And Squashy

I've been soft all my life.
I sound as silent as a mouse.
I am as soft as fur.
You can cuddle me when you are asleep.
I can send you to sleep by magic.
Don't sit on me because I might split open
and all my stuffing will come out.
What am I?

Answer: A teddy bear.

Ruby Mai Dean (6)
Bramley St Peter's CE (VC) Primary School, Bramley

Helpful Technology

Don't use me in the rain
because I will break down.
I am good for playing games on.
You can type anything in me.
You use me when I am on charge.
When I am broken your dad fixes me.
I feel very smooth
but all my keys are bumpy.
What am I?

Answer: A computer.

Lennon Preskey (7)
Bramley St Peter's CE (VC) Primary School, Bramley

A Good Day For Me!

Pet me when I am sad.
Feed me when I am hungry.
Don't forget to give me some water
when I am thirsty.
Don't squeeze me or I will bark.
I feel as fluffy as a teddy bear.
When I am sleepy I curl up
like a hedgehog on the bed.
What am I?

Answer: A dog.

Scarlett Rose Owen (6)
Bramley St Peter's CE (VC) Primary School, Bramley

Flash Bash

Adopt me because I am small.
I am good for playing but I can bite you.
You can get me in all sorts of colours.
Don't get me giddy
because I will run around like mad.
I feel like a pillow and a blanket.
I have a great kennel.
What am I?

Answer: A puppy.

Callum Haigh (7)
Bramley St Peter's CE (VC) Primary School, Bramley

Drinking Nectar

Watch me fly through the jungle.
I feel scaly like a lizard.
Don't go near me even though I'm cute.
Don't annoy me when I am drinking nectar.
When I'm scared I fly away.
My wings rotate in an eight shape.
What am I?

Answer: A hummingbird.

Edgar Cundy
Bramley St Peter's CE (VC) Primary School, Bramley

Nibble And Squeak

Give me lots of water and food.
I am black, brown, grey and white.
I need a big cage because
I have lots of babies.
I sound like a mouse.
My food is brown and sometimes green.
Make sure you stroke me gently.
What am I?

Answer: A guinea pig.

Imogen Martin (7)
Bramley St Peter's CE (VC) Primary School, Bramley

A Sting In The Tail!

Move quietly because I am dangerous.
I have sharp claws like a lobster.
You can find me in lots of habitats.
I come in different colours.
If you come close I will hurt you.
Do not adopt me because I am dangerous.
What am I?

Answer: A scorpion.

Anna Chandler (7)
Bramley St Peter's CE (VC) Primary School, Bramley

Fixer

I am pointy like a knife.
I am good for building with.
Don't let children use me.
Don't press me into your finger
because I am sharp.
I go around and in wood.
Use me to fix things when they fall apart.
What am I?

Answer: A screw.

Kyle Johnson (7)
Bramley St Peter's CE (VC) Primary School, Bramley

Sweet Dreams

I am good for sleeping on.
Use me when you're downstairs
watching TV.
I can come in all shapes and sizes.
I am good for your neck.
I can come in different colours and patterns.
I feel as soft as a cloud.
What am I?

Answer: A pillow.

Faye Durno (6)
Bramley St Peter's CE (VC) Primary School, Bramley

Wash Wash

I am useful to get rid of the germs.
Use me when you are in the bathroom or kitchen.
I am useful after using the toilet.
I feel hard like a brick.
Use me when you need a drink.
If you need a drink turn me on.
What am I?

Answer: A sink.

Amelia-Leigh Varley
Bramley St Peter's CE (VC) Primary School, Bramley

Super Swimmers

Move away from me
otherwise I will bite your finger off.
I am fussy and cute.
I eat tasty, black fish.
Sometimes I even carry my babies
in my mouth.
I can swim in rivers.
I live on the riverbank.
What am I?

Answer: An otter.

Sofie Gilchrist Osborne-Tucimova (7)
Bramley St Peter's CE (VC) Primary School, Bramley

Furball

Give me food and water.
I feel like a furry teddy bear.
I sound like a quiet motorbike.
Sometimes be careful, I can scratch.
I smell as dirty as the mud.
Use me when you are sad,
I can give you a cuddle.
What am I?

Answer: A cat.

Lotachi Ikunna Oke-Nwosu (7)
Bramley St Peter's CE (VC) Primary School, Bramley

Fluffy Ball

Adopt me, I am the cutest thing.
Sometimes I go out into the streets.
I feel as soft as a pillow.
I come in different colours and patterns.
Sometimes I can get angry.
Don't come near me I get scared.
What am I?

Answer: A kitten.

Mollie Archer (7)
Bramley St Peter's CE (VC) Primary School, Bramley

Play On

Press the button to turn me on.
Go on me if you're bored.
Don't leave me on charge or I'll blow.
I feel like a hard metal spoon.
I can come in different colours.
Sometimes put me on charge.
What am I?

Answer: A tablet.

Xander Dennis McGurgan (7)
Bramley St Peter's CE (VC) Primary School, Bramley

Bright Flash!

Press me and I'll do something.
Use me when it is dark.
Sometimes I come in black.
I make a click sound when you flick me.
Don't touch me with wet fingers.
When I am on it is easy to see.
What am I?

Answer: A light switch.

Poppy Spinks (6)
Bramley St Peter's CE (VC) Primary School, Bramley

Fish Habitat

I am a good home for fish.
Fill me up with glistening pebbles.
You make me out of plastic, metal or glass.
I am always inside.
My water is warm or cold and bubbly.
If I leak it means I have a hole.
What am I?

Answer: A fish tank.

Dylan Withers (7)
Bramley St Peter's CE (VC) Primary School, Bramley

Stripy Tale

Move away from me
because I could bite you.
I have a stripy tail to camouflage.
I feel as fluffy as a dog.
Sometimes I can live in cities.
I have sharp claws.
I can be a person's pet.
What am I?

Answer: A raccoon.

Maya Vorlicky (7)
Bramley St Peter's CE (VC) Primary School, Bramley

King Of Ice

I can live on high mountains.
I sound like a lion.
I am a wild predator.
Sometimes I hunt by myself.
Usually, when I am first born
I am called a cub.
Don't mess with a big cat.
What am I?

Answer: A snow leopard.

Adam Chmielewski (7)
Bramley St Peter's CE (VC) Primary School, Bramley

Post Power

Use me when you post things.
I always stay in the corner.
I go to different countries.
Usually, I am red and blue.
I am sometimes in postboxes.
Sometimes I have the Queen's head on me.
What am I?

Answer: A stamp.

Albert Henry Langton (7)
Bramley St Peter's CE (VC) Primary School, Bramley

Swish Swoosh

There are lots of types of me.
I have lots of buttons.
I am mostly white.
Check if I am secure.
I make a swish swoosh noise
when you turn me on.
I am big, wide and heavy.
What am I?

Answer: A washing machine.

Logan Lewis Ivory Sutton (6)
Bramley St Peter's CE (VC) Primary School, Bramley

Tick-Tock Time

Tell the time with me.
I have numbers on me.
I can hang on the wall.
If you need me I come in handy.
When I am broken I can be fixed easily.
I sound like *tick-tock, tick-tock*.
What am I?

Answer: A clock.

Isabella Hemingway (6)
Bramley St Peter's CE (VC) Primary School, Bramley

Home Sweet Home

I'm very comfy.
You like to do lots of activities in me.
You watch telly in me.
You eat stuff in me.
You check what time it is in me.
You play things in me.
You sleep in me.
What am I?

Answer: A house.

Ava Fox (6)
Bramley St Peter's CE (VC) Primary School, Bramley

King Of The Forest

Do not go near me or you will be dinner.
I can fly so high you cannot see me.
I feel like the king of the forest.
I'm so big.
I sound as loud as a T-rex.
I was born in a nest.
What am I?

Answer: A dragon.

Cole Hyde (7)
Bramley St Peter's CE (VC) Primary School, Bramley

Bark At My Trunk

My colours are green, red,
yellow and brown.
Animals use me to make their home.
I am rough like sandpaper.
Don't chop me down.
I start from a seed.
I am bushy on top.
What am I?

Answer: A tree.

Rosie Johnstone (6)
Bramley St Peter's CE (VC) Primary School, Bramley

King Of The Rainforest

Don't come near me because I am fast.
Usually, I am black or orange.
I feel like a teddy bear.
I can bite your finger.
I will eat you up entirely.
I have sharp teeth.
What am I?

Answer: A jaguar. (upside down)

Ridley McManus (7)
Bramley St Peter's CE (VC) Primary School, Bramley

Brrr!

I am very, very cold when you open me.
Fill me up with food.
Don't get me warm.
I keep things cold.
Use me when you have cold food.
Sometimes I make a funny sound.
What am I?

Answer: A fridge.

Jack David Dennis Simpson (7)
Bramley St Peter's CE (VC) Primary School, Bramley

Ring Ring!

I feel as hard as wood.
Use me to call your friends.
Make sure you don't smash my screen.
You can play games on me.
I can take pictures.
We come in different makes.
What am I?

Answer: A phone.

Callum Brown (7)
Bramley St Peter's CE (VC) Primary School, Bramley

Screen Time

Switch me on at a plug socket
and when you don't need me switch me off.
I need a mouse to help me.
Use me after school and in school.
My screen has a stand.
What am I?

Answer: A computer.

Harry Oddy (6)
Bramley St Peter's CE (VC) Primary School, Bramley

Furry Bite

Don't mess with me.
I am like an otter.
I am as cute as a rabbit.
If you shout I will run away.
I can get fatter and fatter.
I can bite your finger off.
What am I?

Answer: A ferret.

Luke Sheldon (7)
Bramley St Peter's CE (VC) Primary School, Bramley

Trick Master

Watch me jump over the waves.
I can swim.
I am blue and white.
I am cute.
Feel me and I will feel smooth
like a wooden deck.
My fin helps me to swim.
What am I?

Answer: A dolphin.

Millie-Rose Manning (6)
Bramley St Peter's CE (VC) Primary School, Bramley

Soft And Fuzzy

I am so cuddly.
I am good for bedtime.
I help you fall asleep.
Squeeze me if you are sad.
I make you feel happy.
I have a nose but I can't smell.
What am I?

Answer: A teddy bear.

Lacey Baird (6)
Bramley St Peter's CE (VC) Primary School, Bramley

Super Swinging Tails

Move away or I will bite your fingers off.
I have a long tail.
I have long ears like a fox.
Sometimes I am stripy.
I eat leaves.
I am a good climber.
What am I?

Answer: A raccoon.

Jack Thomas Albert Martin (7)
Bramley St Peter's CE (VC) Primary School, Bramley

Vertical Climb!

I have feet that grip.
I normally have spots.
I can climb vertically.
I eat fluttering moths.
I live in cities.
I am normally blue.
What am I?

Answer: A tokay gecko.

Finlay Cundy
Bramley St Peter's CE (VC) Primary School, Bramley

Furry Ball

Do not move me.
I am furry.
I feel as friendly as a kitten.
I am cute.
I am nice.
When I am mad I bite you.
I smell like smelly meat.
What am I?

Answer: A dog.

Scarlet Davenport (6)
Bramley St Peter's CE (VC) Primary School, Bramley

Sleepy

I feel like a soft cloud.
Use me when you are tired.
You can stay here all night.
What am I?

Answer: A bed.

Kydon Temple (7), Charlie, Junior Smith (6) & Summer Welsh-Hayden
Bramley St Peter's CE (VC) Primary School, Bramley

Ambush

I am a cat but not a pet.
You need a big truck
to take me to the vet.
I have orange stripes,
I also have black.
When I see a buffalo
I like to attack.
If you see me
run very fast
because if you don't
you won't last!
What am I?

Answer: A tiger.

Woody Bainbridge (6)
Gomersal Primary School, Gomersal

Aliya's Riddle

She flies at night
when the sky is bright.
You might see her soon
if there's a full moon.
She uses her wand
to make a pond.
Aliya is her friend
because she knows how to mend
and she likes to fly with her friend.
Who is she?

Answer: Aliya the witch.

Aliya Lane (5)
Gomersal Primary School, Gomersal

Wing Power

I was once a different creature
crawling all around
but now I'm a beautiful flying insect.
I am very colourful
and I like to be toasty hot.
In the daytime, I like to find flowers.
At night-time, I sleep under a leaf.
What am I?

Answer: A butterfly.

Eadie Chambers (5)
Gomersal Primary School, Gomersal

Hot

I provide light but I'm not a candle.
I'm hot but not a bonfire.
I have rays but not an aquarium.
I'm a star but I'm not a celebrity.
I rise in the morning
but I'm not someone getting out of bed.
What am I?

Answer: The sun.

Leighton Ryan-Moorhouse (6)
Gomersal Primary School, Gomersal

Sugary Treats

I come in all shapes and colours.
I am very yummy.
You get me in a pick-and-mix.
You can spend your pocket money on me.
Share me with your friends
but don't eat too many
because I can rot your teeth.
What am I?

Answer: Sweeties.

Lily-Faye Allan (5)
Gomersal Primary School, Gomersal

Rainbow Sparkle

I live in the woods.
My favourite food is sweet treats.
My hair is white and sparkly.
I am a magical animal.
I look a little bit like a horse.
I have a horn on my head.
I have a rainbow mane.
What am I?

Answer: A unicorn.

Amelia Radforth (6)
Gomersal Primary School, Gomersal

The Rose

Some people call my dad crazy.
I have a pet horse.
My favourite thing to do is read books.
I have a yellow dress.
My best friends are a candle,
teapot and clock.
I have brown hair.
Who am I?

Answer: Belle.

Phoebe Tate (5)
Gomersal Primary School, Gomersal

Gooey, Gooey, Gooey

I am sticky like a bun.
To play with I am fun.
Many colours I can be.
Some people don't like to feel me.
When you squash me I trump.
In the film, I make the Ghostbusters jump.
What am I?

Answer: Slime.

Daniel Eric Booker (6)
Gomersal Primary School, Gomersal

Kick Me!

I am as round as the world.
I come in lots of different colours
and patterns.
I have no sides.
Feet kick me all the time.
If I fly up to the sky
I come back down again.
What am I?

Answer: A football.

Fraser Cowan (6)
Gomersal Primary School, Gomersal

Let's Read Some More

I have a contents page.
I have a blurb.
An illustrator draws my pictures.
An author writes me.
I have a title.
You can read me.
I have chapters.
I have page numbers.
What am I?

Answer: A book.

Matilda May Mills (6)
Gomersal Primary School, Gomersal

Favourite Food

I was made in Italy.
I come in different shapes and sizes
and different colours too.
I can be boiled or baked
and I taste pretty yummy
when covered in tomato sauce.
What am I?

Answer: Pasta.

Grace Emily Sheridan (5)
Gomersal Primary School, Gomersal

A Wriggly Riddle

I am short.
I am long.
I don't make a sound.
I am sort of brown.
I live underground.
I have no eyes
but I can see.
You have to dig to find me.
What am I?

Answer: A worm.

Harry Taylor (5)
Gomersal Primary School, Gomersal

Fast And The Furriest

I am glossy and black.
I love lots of cuddles.
I have won lots of races.
I run very fast
but I love eating and sleeping.
My fur is silky soft.
Who am I?

Answer: Jake the greyhound.

Lucy Alexandra Brown (5)
Gomersal Primary School, Gomersal

A Journey Of Stops And Starts

I have four big wheels.
I can be red.
I can be double or single.
I have windows.
You can sit at the top or bottom.
You pay the driver for your ticket.
What am I?

Answer: A bus.

Daniel Jackson (6)
Gomersal Primary School, Gomersal

Snap, Snap, Snap!

I am dark green.
I am a carnivore.
I live in the sea or rivers.
I've lived in the time of the dinosaurs.
I am a reptile.
I have big teeth.
What am I?

Answer: A crocodile.

Ben Hirst (6)
Gomersal Primary School, Gomersal

Premier League

Lots of people play with it.
People like to watch it.
You can head it.
You can dribble with it.
You can kick it.
You can score with it.
What is it?

Answer: A football.

Noah Williams (6)
Gomersal Primary School, Gomersal

The Sea Tower

I am really tall.
I have lots of steps.
I have a bright light
to guide ships through the night.
I am red and white.
I am near the sea.
What am I?

Answer: A lighthouse.

Harry Hall (5)
Gomersal Primary School, Gomersal

What Am I?

I am a herbivore.
My skin is grey.
I am a mammal.
I live in Africa or Asia.
My baby is a calf.
I play in mud.
I have a horn.
What am I?

Answer: A rhino.

Max Holdsworth (5)
Gomersal Primary School, Gomersal

Treat

I am a circle.
I have a crust.
My favourite topping is pepperoni.
I am eaten in Italy.
I'm eaten hot.
I am very yummy.
What am I?

Answer: A pizza.

Owen Bramwell (5)
Gomersal Primary School, Gomersal

Grizzly Tale

I have a fierce roar.
I have fur.
I live in the forest.
I am a big animal.
I have cubs.
I can go on two or four legs.
What am I?

Answer: A bear.

Isabelle Anders (5)
Gomersal Primary School, Gomersal

Pet

I have to hop.
I have big feet.
I eat carrots.
I am furry.
I have pointy ears.
I have a little tail.
What am I?

Answer: A rabbit.

Lucie Jane Hobson (5)
Gomersal Primary School, Gomersal

Harry's Riddle

I have four legs.
I have a tail.
I have two ears.
I have long hair.
I can carry a passenger.
What am I?

Answer: A horse.

Harry Bradley (6)
Gomersal Primary School, Gomersal

Hunter

I am a cat.
I run fast.
I am fluffy.
I have sharp claws.
I have spots.
I eat meat.
What am I?

Answer: A cheetah.

Isobel Brenda Hobson (5)
Gomersal Primary School, Gomersal

Get In A Spin

I have two feet.
You can spin on me.
I am very tall.
I am lots of fun.
What am I?

Answer: A gymnastics bar.

Paynten-Rose Shaw (6)
Gomersal Primary School, Gomersal

What Has A Neck But No Head?

It is made out of glass.
It has a lid.
It can stand up.
It can roll over.
What is it?

Answer: A bottle.

Edward James Griffiths (5)
Gomersal Primary School, Gomersal

Electric

I have a blue case.
I can play games.
I am portable.
I can FaceTime.
What am I?

Answer: An iPad.

Ethan Bryan (6)
Gomersal Primary School, Gomersal

Beautiful

I can have stripes.
I like flowers.
I start life as a caterpillar.
What am I?

Answer: A butterfly.

Isla-Mai Elizabeth Hutton (5)
Gomersal Primary School, Gomersal

My Riddle

I can come in any size or shape.
I can have lots of flavours.
I look colourful with all my decorations.
You can eat me at a party.
I sometimes have candles on me.
You can buy me from the shops
or bake me at home.
What am I?

Answer: A cake.

Aamilah Bhana (6), Maya Ali & Ezan Abbas
Healey Junior, Infant & Nursery School, Batley

My Riddle

I can come in any shape.
I sometimes will be yummy.
You can have me for a party and for tea.
I get put in an oven.
I look light and bright.
You can put icing on me.
What am I?

Answer: A cake.

Sameeha Rajah (6)
Healey Junior, Infant & Nursery School, Batley

My Riddle

I can come in any shape.
I taste very yummy.
I sometimes have candles on me.
I get put in the oven.
You can have me at a party.
I am yummy and sweet.
What am I?

Answer: A cake.

Miley Hanson-Senior (6)
Healey Junior, Infant & Nursery School, Batley

My Riddle

I am brown all over.
I like playing with my bone.
I like playing with my sticks.
I have furry legs.
I can make a sound.
I like going for a walk.
What am I?

Answer: A dog.

Brooke Aubrey (6)
Healey Junior, Infant & Nursery School, Batley

My Riddle

I have powers.
I have fireballs.
I have blue dungarees.
I have a red hat with an 'M' on it.
I have a best friend.
I have brown shoes.
Who am I?

Answer: Mario.

Zaid Ahmed Bhamji (5)
Healey Junior, Infant & Nursery School, Batley

My Riddle

I live in the Arctic Circle.
I am big.
I eat seals.
I have sharp claws.
I live on the ice and underwater.
I can stomp on the ground.
What am I?

Answer: A polar bear.

Aleeza Sultan (6)
Healey Junior, Infant & Nursery School, Batley

Who Am I?

I have the power of fireballs.
I wear blue dungarees.
I have a friend called Luigi.
I wear a red hat.
I have a moustache.
I like racing.
Who am I?

Answer: Mario.

Joseph Dylan Fenton (6)
Healey Junior, Infant & Nursery School, Batley

My Riddle

I live in the Arctic.
I eat seeds and plants.
I am white.
I cannot fly.
I have big ears.
I am big.
I have small legs.
What am I?

Answer: An Arctic hare.

Millie Ramsden (5)
Healey Junior, Infant & Nursery School, Batley

My Riddle

I am mostly dark red.
I have spikes on my back.
I breathe fire.
I have a pattern on my back.
I can't talk.
I am an animal.
What am I?

Answer: A dragon.

Aadam Mahmood (5)
Healey Junior, Infant & Nursery School, Batley

My Riddle

I live in the Arctic.
I am small.
I have a tail.
I eat fish.
I am white in the winter
and I am brown in the summer.
What am I?

Answer: An Arctic fox.

Lexie Leigh Trott (6)
Healey Junior, Infant & Nursery School, Batley

My Riddle

I have eight legs.
I am hairy.
I can be black or brown.
I can be big or small.
I can climb up walls.
I can crawl.
What am I?

Answer: A spider.

Mason Massey (6)
Healey Junior, Infant & Nursery School, Batley

My Riddle

I wear a red hat.
I wear blue dungarees.
I have a moustache.
I have brown shoes.
I have a friend called Princess Peach.
Who am I?

Answer: Mario.

Maxie Mir (6)
Healey Junior, Infant & Nursery School, Batley

My Riddle

I am big.
I have flippers.
I have a beak.
I am black and white.
I eat fish and squid.
I live in the Arctic.
What am I?

Answer: A penguin.

Zain Masood Lunat (5)
Healey Junior, Infant & Nursery School, Batley

My Riddle

I have a best friend called Luigi.
I wear a red hat.
I wear blue dungarees.
I have brown shoes.
I like racing.
Who am I?

Answer: Mario.

Ayaan Hussain (6)
Healey Junior, Infant & Nursery School, Batley

My Riddle

I live in the Arctic Circle.
I eat fish and squid.
I have flippers.
I am small.
I am black and white.
What am I?

Answer: A penguin.

Shahir Hussain Ahmed (5)
Healey Junior, Infant & Nursery School, Batley

My Riddle

I live in the Arctic.
I am big.
I have tusks.
I eat fish.
I live in the water.
I have body fat.
What am I?

Answer: A walrus.

Delisia Docherty (6)
Healey Junior, Infant & Nursery School, Batley

My Riddle

I am big.
I live in the Arctic.
I have a small head.
I eat fish.
I live on land.
I have a tail.
What am I?

Answer: A Husky.

Rhys James Bingham (6)
Healey Junior, Infant & Nursery School, Batley

My Riddle

I am red and blue.
I have spikes.
I have two wings.
I have sharp, pointy teeth.
I breathe fire.
What am I?

Answer: A dragon.

Harris Tariq Hanif (6)
Healey Junior, Infant & Nursery School, Batley

My Riddle

I live under the sea.
I am blue.
I have sharp teeth.
I am big.
I have a long tail.
I bite.
What am I?

Answer: A shark.

Ayaan Hussain (6)
Healey Junior, Infant & Nursery School, Batley

My Riddle

I have whiskers.
I live in the Arctic.
I eat fish.
I am big.
I live in the sea.
I am white.
What am I?

Answer: A seal.

Zaara Raja (5)
Healey Junior, Infant & Nursery School, Batley

My Riddle

I eat fish.
I am big.
I swim.
I lie in the snow.
I live in the Arctic.
What am I?

Answer: A polar bear.

Maison Reynard (5)
Healey Junior, Infant & Nursery School, Batley

My Riddle

I have soft fur.
I like to drink milk.
I have a tail.
I make a sound.
What am I?

Answer: A cat.

Tillie Lowrie (6)
Healey Junior, Infant & Nursery School, Batley

My Riddle

I am white.
I live in the Arctic.
I eat fish.
I have flippers.
What am I?

Answer: A penguin.

Riley Robin North (5)
Healey Junior, Infant & Nursery School, Batley

My Riddle

I live in the Arctic.
I eat fish.
I have big eyes.
What am I?

Answer: A polar bear.

Aqsa Younus Raja (5)
Healey Junior, Infant & Nursery School, Batley

Aeroplane Maker

It can be different colours.
It has four corners.
It's got four sides.
You can cut it.
You can make an aeroplane with it.
It's white most of the time.
What is it?

Answer: Paper.

Fathima Hussain (7)
Home Schooled, Halifax

The Colourful Door

It has a window.
It has a door.
It has a handle.
It has curtains.
It has a path.
What is it?

Answer: A house.

Zaynab Hussain (6)
Home Schooled, Halifax

I'm Not Friendly

I have pointy ears.
Scariness and I come out in the night.
I have powers and hate people.
I have squeaky friends that fly at night.
I have good, outstanding
and fantastic hearing.
I am dark, dull and dark red everywhere.
I have white skin.
It is very thin and smooth.
I like to drink red juice everywhere I am.
What am I?

Answer: A vampire.

Isa Tilal (7)
Lidget Green Primary School, Lidget Green

The Angry Wing

I have glorious wings.
I can fly like a bird.
I have a lovely white cloak and white wings.
I look beautiful.
I look just like a fairy or similar.
I told Mary that she was going to have a baby named Jesus.
I can fly upside down.
I have somebody to help me all the time.
I look like a butterfly but I'm not.
What am I?

Answer: An angel.

Aliyah Ali Hussain (7)
Lidget Green Primary School, Lidget Green

My Favourite Fruit

I am bright, wrinkled and red.
I have green, straight and floppy things.
I am pointy at the bottom
and smooth at the top.
I am not human, I live in a fruit bowl.
I cannot move unless someone picks me up.
I can be eaten slow or quick.
What am I?

Answer: A strawberry.

Zainab Batool (7)
Lidget Green Primary School, Lidget Green

Sunny Summer

I am yellow.
I shine bright in summer.
I am round, not a sphere.
I am for summer,
You don't need me every day, do you?
I am big, round
And too sunny for you.
I have seven pointy edges.
I begin with an 'S'.
What am I?

Answer: *The sun.*

Inaya Zara Moghul (7)
Lidget Green Primary School, Lidget Green

Furry Tail

My animal is furry.
My animal is gorgeous.
My animal is kind.
My animal is nice.
My animal is cool.
My animal has furry ears.
My animal is fluffy.
My animal is a furry tail.
My animal is cuddly and brown.
What is it?

Answer: A rabbit.

Muskaan Karim (6)
Lidget Green Primary School, Lidget Green

White Arctic Animal

I have a black nose.
I have white fur.
I am like a panda but bigger.
My fur is all white.
I live near the North Pole.
I'm the furthest away from the Equator.
I'm a meat eater.
I like fish.
What am I?

Answer: A polar bear.

Israr Ali Shah (7)
Lidget Green Primary School, Lidget Green

Fierce Frights

My skin is stripy, strong and fierce.
My ears are floppy, soft and thin.
My tail is fluffy, cuddly and furry.
My legs are slippy, wobbly and rocky.
My eyes are blue and scary.
What am I?

Answer: A tiger.

Rayyan Nazir (7)
Lidget Green Primary School, Lidget Green

Hop Up And Down

I can hop up and down with my short feet.
My favourite food is orange carrots.
I have long, brown and silky whiskers.
I have fluffy fur.
I could be white, black or grey.
What am I?

Answer: A rabbit.

Rabiya Lateef (7)
Lidget Green Primary School, Lidget Green

Flame Breather

I have sharp teeth and I am loud.
I am rough like a tree.
I have sharp claws but not feet.
I have big, fat feet.
I am as big as an elephant.
What am I?

Answer: A dinosaur.

Ahmad Raza (7)
Lidget Green Primary School, Lidget Green

Healthy Teeth

I check people's teeth.
I give you fillings.
I can count your teeth.
I have a partner.
I have blue clothes.
I give you water.
Who am I?

Answer: A dentist.

Anmol Zeb (6)
Lidget Green Primary School, Lidget Green

Magical Wings

I am beautiful, colourful and bright.
My glowing wings really love the sun.
My food comes from flowers
and is super yummy.
I use my long tongue to fill my tummy.
You can meet me in your garden
when it is hot and sunny.
You have a chance to catch me
if you are as fast as a bunny.
What am I?

Answer: A butterfly.

Nicole Getka (7)
Morley Newlands Academy, Morley

Race!

I have big black wheels.
I have fancy paintwork on me.
I can jump up high in the air.
I can do front flips and back flips in the air.
I am black and orange.
What am I?

Answer: A monster truck.

Jack Smith (7)
Morley Newlands Academy, Morley

Jungle Book

I have wet, moist skin.
I live on land and in water.
I slither around the wild forest
with my wild friends.
I also have some scales too.
What am I?

Answer: A snake.

Arissa Comrie (7)
Morley Newlands Academy, Morley

Fluffy

I eat biscuits.
I have four legs.
I have long whiskers.
I have a tail.
I can see at night.
I can jump.
I can miaow.
What am I?

Answer: A cat.

Amie Bruniges (5)
Old Bank Junior Infant & Nursery School, Mirfield

The Arctic

I live in the Arctic.
I can waddle.
I am black.
I have blue eyes.
I have orange feet.
I carry eggs on my feet.
What am I?

Answer: A penguin.

Aleksander Kusek (6)
Old Bank Junior Infant & Nursery School, Mirfield

In The Deep

I live in water.
I have sharp teeth.
I am not friendly.
I can swim fast.
I have no legs.
I have fins.
What am I?

Answer: A shark.

Jamie Lucas McKay (5)
Old Bank Junior Infant & Nursery School, Mirfield

Flutter

I have wings.
I can fly.
I like flowers.
I am colourful.
I am pretty.
I can be big or small.
What am I?

Answer: A butterfly.

Jasmine Baker (6)
Old Bank Junior Infant & Nursery School, Mirfield

At The Deep

I have sharp teeth.
I live in water.
I have no legs.
I can swim.
I have fins.
I am mean.
What am I?

Answer: A shark.

Isaac Wood-Carney (5)
Old Bank Junior Infant & Nursery School, Mirfield

Sea Monster

I have no legs.
I have got a big mouth.
I have big teeth.
I have got big eyes.
I can swim.
What am I?

Answer: A shark.

Harrison Joe Reynolds (6)
Old Bank Junior Infant & Nursery School, Mirfield

Under The Sea

I have eight legs.
I live in water.
I am wobbly.
I can stick to things.
I am purple.
What am I?

Answer: An octopus.

Alexandra Nagy (5)
Old Bank Junior Infant & Nursery School, Mirfield

Snappy

I live in water.
I have a tail.
I have spikes.
I have big teeth.
I have big eyes.
What am I?

Answer: A crocodile.

Ethan Newby (5)
Old Bank Junior Infant & Nursery School, Mirfield

Slither

I am poisonous.
I stick my tongue out.
I slither.
I gulp my food down.
I go up trees.
What am I?

Answer: A snake.

Isaac Whitfield (5)
Old Bank Junior Infant & Nursery School, Mirfield

Splash

I have no legs.
I can swim.
I have sharp teeth.
I can dive.
I live in water.
What am I?

Answer: A shark.

Zach Shackleton (6)
Old Bank Junior Infant & Nursery School, Mirfield

Clip-Clop

I have four legs.
I eat hay.
I have hair.
I live on a farm.
I go clip-clop.
What am I?

Answer: A horse.

Lexi Kim Main (6)
Old Bank Junior Infant & Nursery School, Mirfield

What Am I?

I am soft.
I have four legs.
I have ears.
I have a soft tail.
I am an animal.
What am I?

Answer: A dog.

Lyla Buckley (5)
Old Bank Junior Infant & Nursery School, Mirfield

I Like Food

I have four paws.
I have a tail.
I can miaow.
I can run.
I live in a house.
What am I?

Answer: A cat.

Eirlys Tomlinson (6)
Old Bank Junior Infant & Nursery School, Mirfield

In The Web

I have eight legs.
I can crawl.
I can bite.
I can spin silk.
I am small.
What am I?

Answer: A spider.

Deakon Lucas Clayton (6)
Old Bank Junior Infant & Nursery School, Mirfield

Swimmer

I have no legs.
I have some teeth.
I make a pop sound.
I can swim.
What am I?

Answer: A fish.

Klisha Khan (6)
Old Bank Junior Infant & Nursery School, Mirfield

Jungle King

I can roar.
I have four legs.
I have a soft tail.
I can stamp.
What am I?

Answer: A tiger.

Ajie Humma (5)
Old Bank Junior Infant & Nursery School, Mirfield

Heavenly Snack

I am a type of moon shape.
I am so yummy
that you would like to eat me.
I am a healthy fruit.
I am yellow.
I am so long.
I am not alive right now.
I am sometimes green
when I am not ripe.
What am I?

Answer: A banana.

Ryan Cornelius Lloyd (6)
Our Lady Of Lourdes Catholic Primary School, Sheepridge

The Fastest Of All

I am strong enough to hold four people.
You can go for miles.
I can take my roof off.
I am really fast.
I am not alive.
I can take people for rides.
What am I?

Answer: A car.

Rhylee Phillips
Our Lady Of Lourdes Catholic Primary School, Sheepridge

Healthy Snack

I am a type of moon shape.
I am so yummy that someone would eat me.
I am very healthy.
I am not alive.
I am yellow.
I am the best taste ever.
What am I?

Answer: A banana.

Isaac Ashish Lazarus (6)
Our Lady Of Lourdes Catholic Primary School, Sheepridge

Fastest Of All

I can be any colour.
I can help people get to school.
I can go very fast.
I can park somewhere.
I have four wheels.
I have windows.
What am I?

Answer: A car.

Nicol Katarzyna Domanska (5)
Our Lady Of Lourdes Catholic Primary School, Sheepridge

I Am Tall And Small

I am tall and small.
I can be green and red.
You can find me outside.
I have lots of arms.
I need water and sun to live.
What am I?

Answer: A tree.

Nadia, Tianna Morgan, Amelia & Tomasz
Our Lady Of Lourdes Catholic Primary School, Sheepridge

Fast Vehicles

It is not living but it moves.
It has four wheels.
It has windows in it.
It can be different colours.
It can go fast.
What is it?

Answer: A car.

Kyrelle Wood (6)
Our Lady Of Lourdes Catholic Primary School, Sheepridge

A Fluttery Creature

I am extremely small.
I have beady eyes as small as a ladybird.
Sadly, I look like a glow-worm
when I'm on the ground.
Unluckily I am as small
as a blade of green grass.
I fly as high as the fluffy clouds.
If you don't listen carefully
you won't hear my silvery and soft voice.
What am I?

Answer: A fairy.

Humayra Patel (8)
Paradise Primary School, Savile Town

A Tool's Blood

I have blood inside me.
I am mostly used in English and maths.
I have a lid so I don't get dry.
If I don't have blood I don't work anymore.
My blood comes in different colours,
sometimes red and sometimes blue
and in all the colours of the rainbow too.
I am used by a lot of people.
What am I?

Answer: A pen.

Aisha Bodhania (7)
Paradise Primary School, Savile Town

The Shining Stone

I come in lots of different shapes.
I am sometimes the colour
of light, red blood,
fresh green grass,
or the shimmering ocean.
I shine like the shining sun.
I am kept safe in a beautiful case.
I live in deep mines.
Sometimes I am worth more than gold
and sometimes I am not.
What am I?

Answer: A gem.

Muhammad Muaaz Ismail (8)
Paradise Primary School, Savile Town

The Gigantic Giant

My neck is as massive as a skyscraper.
I like to walk as slow as a tortoise.
I eat from trees that don't have branches.
I am a herbivore.
Some people are scared when I bite.
Sometimes I think I'm a giant.
I am the tallest dinosaur that ever lived.
What am I?

Answer: A brachiosaurus.

Muhammad Soyab Patel (8)
Paradise Primary School, Savile Town

The Noisy Flyer

I am bright and colourful.
My beak is as black as a bear.
I have a long, beautiful beak.
I am mostly sold to old people.
I live in the jungle
but people find me
and take me to Pets at Home.
I copy everyone whatever they say.
What am I?

Answer: A noisy parrot.

Maryam Polli (8)
Paradise Primary School, Savile Town

A Cute Pet

I have nice, fluffy fur.
I have sharp, shark teeth.
I eat something
that eats nice yellow cheese.
I hate see-through, wet, cold stuff on me.
I have prickly whiskers.
I love gentle pats on my back.
What am I?

Answer: A cat.

Umaama Ali (8)
Paradise Primary School, Savile Town

In The Deep

People like to spy on me.
I have sharp teeth.
I can be dangerous.
I love to eat fish.
I don't live in any country.
I swim really fast.
People are scared of me.
What am I?

Answer: A shark.

Hafsa Tukur (8)
Paradise Primary School, Savile Town

The Speed Of Light

I run as fast as light.
I am a big, bad cat.
I am very fluffy like a bunny.
I'm very mean when I'm seen.
I hunt for my prey.
I get eaten by a tiger or a lion.
What am I?

Answer: A cheetah.

Fatima Moosa (8)
Paradise Primary School, Savile Town

My Red Ruby

I am as red as a ruby.
My leaves are so spiky and green.
My black seeds are as black as ebony.
I am so juicy.
I am very, very healthy.
I am a type of fruit.
What am I?

Answer: A strawberry.

Maariyah Moosa (7)
Paradise Primary School, Savile Town

The Terrifying Eater

I am a meat eater.
I have a big furry mane.
I have sharp nails.
I have sharp teeth.
I am the king of the jungle.
I am so terrifying.
What am I?

Answer: A lion.

Ariana Razaq (8)
Paradise Primary School, Savile Town

The Brave Girl

She lived in a house made of wood.
She was a girl.
She had two plaits in her hair.
She went to see the Wizard of Oz.
She had a scarecrow friend.
She had brown hair.
She followed the yellow brick road.
She was very brave.
She made lots of friends.
She had a dog called Toto.
Her home was in Kansas.
Who was she?

Answer: Dorothy.

Hannah Plant (6)
Southroyd Primary School, Pudsey

Huddle

I am a bird but I can't fly.
I prefer the water rather than the sky.
I'm covered in down that's black and white
and can lay eggs day or night.
I like to swim so I live near the sea.
I eat lots of fish for my tea.
What am I?

Answer: A penguin.

Dylan James Hall (6)
Southroyd Primary School, Pudsey

Crazy Racing

Up and down the hill I go.
Straight on the flat
and a corner to follow.
Cars can go fast
but I don't allow bikes.
Crash on the bend
can end in the barriers.
What am I?

Answer: A racing track.

Henrikas Merkelis (5)
Southroyd Primary School, Pudsey

Ton And Not

I am a word with three letters.
The number of consonants I have is two.
I have one vowel too.
Write me down, I am a lot.
Back to front, I am not.
What am I?

Answer: Ton.

Eleanor Ighayere (6)
Southroyd Primary School, Pudsey

Who Am I?

I have two eyes.
I have hair.
I am a mammal.
I have arms.
I have two legs
and a bottom.
Who am I?

Answer: A person.

Lauren Bayly (6)
Southroyd Primary School, Pudsey

An Icy Island Animal

I am as cold as a winter night.
I live in an icy house.
I'm not that warm after all.
I walk differently than other animals.
I have a lot of friends
that swim like me.
My parents do a lot for me
like regurgitating food and looking after me.
I have quite a long beak
which helps me to catch my prey.
My belly is white
and my flippers are black
so my friends can find me
when I am out in the icy waves
and when I am near predators.
What am I?

Answer: A penguin.

Ruby Smith (9)
St Luke's CE Primary School, Bradford

Sharp Claws

I have teeth as sharp as a blade.
I jump far distances.
I roam in the wild.
I hate water.
I warn my prey with a scary roar.
I am a meat eater.
I am not a pet.
I am a good climber.
I can sleep in a cave.
I also roam in the snowy forests.
What am I?

Answer: A snow leopard.

Mia Pheasby (10)
St Luke's CE Primary School, Bradford

Flying Colours

I am used on a certain day of the year.
Sometimes I am used for birthday parties.
There are loads of different colours of me.
Don't go near me, I will burn you.
Cover your ears, I am very loud.
What am I?

Answer: Fireworks.

Sophie Grace Crabtree (9)
St Luke's CE Primary School, Bradford

The Food Stealer

I soar through the bright blue sky.
I stay near water.
If any of my bird friends have food
I will attack them for it.
I have a long yellow beak.
I am very cheeky.
I may steal your food.
What am I?

Answer: A seagull.

Ray Henry Mathieson (9)
St Luke's CE Primary School, Bradford

As Fast As Lightning

My rev is as loud as a lion's roar.
I am as fast as a cheetah.
I drift around corners amazingly.
I am a popular car.
I am not easy to afford.
I might even be your dream car.
What am I?

Answer: A Ferrari.

Darnell Blythe (10)
St Luke's CE Primary School, Bradford

Grass Grower

I am as red as fire.
Using sun and rain can help me to live.
I'm used as a gift.
Creatures collect something from me.
Some people are allergic to me.
I grow in the grass.
What am I?

Answer: A rose.

Shola Henderson (9)
St Luke's CE Primary School, Bradford

Castle Destroyer

I have yellow fluorescent spikes
all over my back.
I have gigantic beady eyes.
I can fly as high as the clouds.
I breathe scorching fire.
I am as ginormous as a bus.
What am I?

Answer: A dragon.

Daniel Senior (9)
St Luke's CE Primary School, Bradford

Higher Than The Clouds

I can be anywhere.
You cannot touch me.
I go higher than the clouds.
I only come when it rains and is sunny.
I am beautiful.
I have colours.
I have treasure.
What am I?

Answer: A rainbow.

Grace Mitchell (10)
St Luke's CE Primary School, Bradford

Cooling You Down

I'm used in hot weathers.
I am as shiny as iron.
Electricity powers me.
I have a metal bar around my head.
I have a dangerous blade.
I create wind as cool as ice.
What am I?

Answer: A fan.

Thomas Pashley (10)
St Luke's CE Primary School, Bradford

A Black Furball

I jump, I like playing out.
I jump at my owner and scream.
I'm black, I'm furry
and I have a pink nose.
I'm wild sometimes.
I scratch like a predator.
What am I?

Answer: A kitten.

Tyler Rhodes (9)
St Luke's CE Primary School, Bradford

Stripe

I have stripes on my back.
I sleep in the wild.
I have sharp teeth.
I can be in the zoo.
Sometimes I'm lazy but not all the time.
I'm black and orange.
What am I?

Answer: A tiger.

Daniela Megija Cielava (9)
St Luke's CE Primary School, Bradford

Melody As Long As Time

I've been around forever.
You cannot see me but you can hear me.
I'm the most beautiful thing ever.
I can be used in conversation.
I have no heartbeat.
What am I?

Answer: A voice.

Lily Robinson (10)
St Luke's CE Primary School, Bradford

Can You Spot The Animal?

I am as fast as a car.
I am a carnivore and hunt for my prey.
I am the fastest land animal.
I have a beastly roar.
I am a gorilla's worst enemy.
What am I?

Answer: A cheetah.

Rayaan Ahmed Ali (9)
St Luke's CE Primary School, Bradford

The Sloppy Gloppy Mess

I am very sloppy and sticky.
I come in different colours.
I get poked a lot.
I can come large or small.
I am very stretchy.
What am I?

Answer: Slime.

Grace Hutchinson (10)
St Luke's CE Primary School, Bradford

YOUNG WRITERS INFORMATION

We hope you have enjoyed reading this book – and that you will continue to in the coming years.

If you're a young writer who enjoys reading and creative writing, or the parent of an enthusiastic poet or story writer, do visit our website **www.youngwriters.co.uk**. Here you will find free competitions, workshops and games, as well as recommended reads, a poetry glossary and our blog.

If you would like to order further copies of this book, or any of our other titles, then please give us a call or visit **www.youngwriters.co.uk**.

Young Writers
Remus House
Coltsfoot Drive
Peterborough
PE2 9BF
(01733) 890066
info@youngwriters.co.uk